Love From an Airplane Window

Dedication

For Alex, the very first person who stole my heart while traveling. From 2007 to now, from the east coast to the west, I've loved every minute of adventuring with you.

For my parents, for intentionally instilling in me a deep love of literature and travel from an incredibly young age. I love you beyond words.

Preface

Travel and adventure have always been huge parts of my life. Since boarding a plane for the first time at six months old, I've traveled non-stop since; I even once made a career out of it as a travel agent! I've been blessed to spend a lot of time away from sweet home Chicago, seeing many beautiful places and meeting—and falling in love with—many beautiful people.

After my very first solo trip at fifteen, it didn't take me long to realize that being both a wanderer and a hopeless romantic was not, in fact, the ideal combination. Over the years, my heart has been scattered throughout the world; its pieces held by many people—some I have regular contact with, and some I will never see again. Making the conscious choice to date while away from home is unconventional at best, I'm aware. I'm a better person for it, though. I've met many wonderful people, experienced many cultures, and gotten the chance to have adventures I wouldn't normally have.

Unfortunately, the goodbyes that follow are much harder than the *see you later* I typically say to a place or a person. It's different when I know I'm leaving behind a piece of my heart with someone, unsure of what—if anything—the future holds once I get on that airplane. Having dated in such a way, it makes it difficult to date "normally" at home because it isn't as intense as I'm used to while traveling.

I've taken this past year and a half of travel and dating to really sit down with myself and examine what each of those means to me and what they look like in my life, both together and separate. When I asked myself what I thought they meant, the word *home* came to me. It's easy for me to find myself at home in a place I love, or in a new place I find myself falling in love with. It's easy for me to picture what my life would look like there. I know, though, that ultimately where I will call home isn't a where at all, but *whom*. I suppose that's why I date and travel simultaneously; I don't care where I end up as long as I'm with the person who is home. I'm a wanderer—I can make my home anywhere as long as the right person is by my side.

And when yours fails,
I will be your strength.

Come home to me,

and let yourself be loved.

Every page,

every word,

is bringing you back to me.

—wishful thinking

Please,

just let me be your safe harbor.

Thank you.

For staying.

—even when it's hard

That's the thing about lasts—

they never come with a warning.

Maybe—

just maybe—

if I don't write about it,

it won't be real,

and you won't leave . . .

—right?

Held by him

but feeling your arms.

—a battle I never wanted to fight

I could've loved you

just a little bit

(forever)

longer.

A simple truth,

a painful truth:

I will always love you.

It will always be you.

Losing you

is a losing battle.

If I'd only known

that last time was the last time,

I wouldn't have let you rush—

I would've held you

a little closer,

a little tighter,

a little longer . . .

And kissed you just one more time.

The stars shined like something out of a fairy tale,

and for a moment,

you were mine.

—love under Oregon skies

You love parts of me
that I didn't even know existed
to be loved.

I guess these pages

will always be my one great

(final)

love letter to you.

To me,

every word

sounds like your name.

I've come to terms with the fact
that I'll be writing about you forever,
until I find myself searching for you
in our next lifetime.

Suddenly,
it hit me:

You're gone
and not coming back.

—endings

I'll always wonder

if you've read what's yours.

—guess I'll never know

You

are a new kind of loss

that I never saw coming.

I fell in love with you

the same way you left me:

All at once

and in a way that changed my life

forever.

Promise me this,
my girl:

That you will never again beg someone
to see the worth
that is embedded in your soul.

That you will never again beg someone
to love you.

Someday,

I will open my arms

and say,

"welcome home."

You wrap me in your arms,

pulling me closer with every heartbeat—

this is coming home.

What an honor it is

to love you through every lifetime.

I will love you forever,

if for no other reason than

I do not know how not to.

Let this second chance

not be wasted on fear,

but rooted in a love

so deeply sown

in the beauty of it all.

I whisper your name to the stars

and watch them illuminate the sky

For the world to bask in your beauty.

You

make me dizzy

with desire.

Wait—

I'm not done making memories with you.

Tomorrow is not promised—

I will love you enough

today

to carry us through

our next lifetime together.

I bury my face in your shoulder

and inhale the sweet scent

of coming home.

You

are a beautiful, new hope.

You.

Me.

Us.

Forever.

—all in

At the end of the day,
I still couldn't be
more thankful
for you.

Time

has yet to dry these tears . . .

Once again,

I'm being pulled back

into you

—g r a v i t y

At the end of the day,

you

were supposed to be

my forever.

Your voice—

it brings me back every time.

I close my eyes,
and you're here.
And I'm home.

You
are everything I love
about this city I call home.

—Chicago

Promise me

that you will always love me

first.

Will

love

ever be unaccompanied by

fear?

—wondering

You

are the greatest love of my life.

You make it so easy

to count my blessings.

—abundance

I will build you a home in these arms;

they will never let you go.

I just thought—

maybe—

it was you.

And when you left,

you took my whole heart with you.

Try as I may,

I'll never forget

the way you held me.

The hours

turn into days,

turn into nights,

and you're still gone.

I hope you know
it'll always be you.

Please,

don't let me go.

Let me stay in this one last moment

just a little

(forever)

longer.

I promise to love you

even when I can't remember.

We will plant our roots

in each other.

—growth

Life just makes more sense
with you.

Love—

what a special kind of

h e a v e n ,

what a special kind of

h e l l .

Once again,

I fall asleep to the sweet sting

of you . . .

There are so many things

I wish I could tell you.

Instead,

I'll tell my stories to the stars

and hope they whisper

it all back to you.

This time,

after I pull you into me again

closer

closer

closer,

I will let you go . . .

—more wishful thinking

To leave a place is one thing,
but to leave behind a person—
that's something else altogether.

Something so heartbreakingly beautiful
that the words on these pages
simply can't touch it.

—Nevada

My dear,

I pray you never know

the special type of pain

that is leaving behind a love.

And on that day—

that hot Friday afternoon—

I left behind a part of my heart

that I knew I was never getting back.

—falling in love from an airplane window

Take me back

to that desert oasis—

where I can once again feel my feet in the water,

taste that cold coffee with the heat on my back,

see those beautiful blue eyes beside me,

and know I'm home.

—the lake

I wrote about you today.

I wrote about
lakes
and blue eyes
and iced coffee.

I wrote about
late nights,
first kisses,
the desert,
country music,
and chance meetings.

I wrote about
flying,
falling,
and gambling my heart on 1,723 miles.

I wrote about you today,
and just for a moment,
you were here.

I fell

as you flew;

but if you fall too,

I'll always fly back to you.

I see your face
in the cracks of sunlight.

In the summer heat,
I feel your arms.

I see your blue eyes
in that beautiful, clear sky.

—you are everywhere

Hope—

what a dangerously terrifying idea.

The moment I knew

that I wasn't getting this part of my heart back

was very same moment

I started writing about you.

Falling in love while traveling
is a special kind of torture.

To simultaneously be
a wanderer
and a hopeless romantic
means my heart is scattered
from sea to shining sea,
leaving behind pieces I'll never recover.

The stars,

the universe,

and time

all aligned

the first time your eyes met mine.

The sunlight dancing on your hair,

reflecting off the lake,

illuminating those blue eyes—

I knew then

that I would find myself

writing about you.

Is it so crazy to think

that we've met in some other lifetime?

That this is the second chance we once begged the universe for?

The way your hand
so perfectly fits in mine.

The way my head
lands perfectly on your heart
when you hold me close.

The way your voice
brings calm
in this crazy city.

The way we talk
as if we've known each other forever.

—our souls just knew

I will always tell you
why I chose you.

—fear not

There simply isn't enough time

to hold you so tightly

for the last time.

—airport goodbyes

For a moment,
as we sat on that mountain
overlooking the city,
I called you mine.

And in that moment,
we were eternal.

—just a moment

Wherever you are,

I hope the sun shines bright

and the wind is still

and something makes you miss me.

I look to the clouds

and pray

that you're looking down at me.

—flight

You instantly became

my greatest adventure.

I find myself

counting clouds

and counting days.

You taste like Las Vegas—

like chlorine,

sunshine,

tequila,

and love.

So much love.

My heart and mind swirled

like the propeller of your plane—
strong,

powerful—

you blow me away.

Someday,

one of these planes

will land me right back in your arms.

What a beautiful love it must be,

to move mountains like mine.

And oh,

to miss you like this . . .

The larger-than-life fountain danced

to that love song,

and our hearts joined in the beautiful symphony,

a compilation as carefully timed

as the water's miraculous (beautiful) movement.

What a confusing feeling,

to constantly live in this state of both

hope

and doubt.

I will love you like the sun—
it always shines,
even through the darkest of storms.

I will love you like the moon—
it lights up the night
even when you can't see it.

I will love you the way
you deserve to be loved—
unconditionally.

—always

You deserve a love

so strong

that it carries you through

your darkest days.

You deserve a love

so sweet

that it makes you look forward

to each new adventure.

You deserve a love

so unconditional

that you aren't afraid

to be your (wonderful) self.

You deserve a love

so powerfully endless

that you want to live

to see each new day.

I promise

if you hold on long enough

to see tomorrow,

that I will hold you through the night,

and will be waiting at the sunrise

with outstretched arms.

Tell me about your battles,
show me your demons,
and let me pull you into me
and love you harder.

And when I look to the future,

I see your face.

Please let me be your peace

in this world

that I know is not always kind to you.

Let me be your hope

when it's hard to see past today.

Let me be your light

when the night is simply

too dark.

Please,

let me love you.

.

You

are better than my morning coffee.

Fearlessly

is how I intend to love you.

Don't you worry,

this love will prevail.

Soon

your sun will rise,

and I'll be there waiting

at the break of dawn,

ready to reach for your hand.

—take it when you're ready

This is me,

never putting you down.

I wanted to write about you tonight,

but I'm exhausted.

I guess I've simply

used up

all my words meant for you.

—now I'll rest

Try as I may,

making you the villain of our story

will never change the ending.

I will love you forever

and I can only hope

that you're here to see it.

I am not a convenience—

I am a *f o r e v e r.*

Oh honey—

if you ask them to choose,

they won't choose you.

—the other woman

You deserve to be kissed

with a passion

that ignites the long dead *fires*

in your soul

and burns

any doubts

to the ground.

"That spark in your eyes,"

—he asked—

"is it lust or love?"

"Both."

my heart whispered.

I write about you,
and for a moment,
you're mine.

When our adventure here has expired,

and life says that our time is up,

I promise to save

my very last dance

for you.

Have you ever thought
that maybe
it's actually me?

You are deserving of a love

that would move galaxies

for the chance to hold your hand.

One kiss

is all it took

and you had me

h i g h e r

than the Colorado sky.

Never again

will I remove my crown

to fit through your doorway.

You tell me to leave

but squeeze my hand as I do.

If only I'd known

how sharp your edges would become . . .

I would've loved you anyway.

I can't wait for the first time

the sun rises

on a brand new day

and you're still here next to me.

I have loved you

with everything in me,

and I will lose you

the same way.

Just please don't tell me
you love her more.

I pray to God

this wasn't also

the beginning of our end.

Tell me—

in what universe

do we pull this off?

In what timeline

do we get away with this?

Are we ever successful?

In what world

do we manage to fall in love

with each other

without consequence?

Tell me

how the hell

this is supposed to work.

I close my eyes

and I'm right back to kissing you,

under a waterfall,

without 2,100 miles between us

or any cares in the world.

All I know

in this crazy world

is how to hold on to you.

Give me your all

or give me nothing—

I'm too much

to be an in-between.

I don't want heaven
if it doesn't involve you.

Start over with me,
and let's make all our
wildest dreams
come true.

You
are the love song
I never deserved
but will dance to
f o r e v e r.

Life is too

fragile

to sit here

keeping score against you.

—forgiveness

How wonderful it is

to see you

in this whole new light.

Your midnight eyes
and my tangled hair
drowned in the glow
of the distant city lights—
what an adventure
you turned out to be.
And my god,
I'd do it all over again.

—Astoria

"Just friends"

never really sounded right,

did it?

In the heat of the moment,

I caught myself

falling in love with you.

I don't know what we were,

but my god,

we were alive.

Promise me

we'll make the most of this—

rarely does

"right place, wrong time"

get a second chance.

I can't make you love me,

but oh,

if I could.

Do you think that

maybe

this could be the start of some

beautiful eternity?

Change is hard—
promise me
you'll hold my hand
through it all.

—growing pains

Tell me—

how do I navigate this world

without my muse?

—mourning

I will not allow

another woman

to walk through the same

hellfire

that burned me.

How do you write

about a world gone dark?

And when you hear that song,

I can only hope that—

maybe—

you'll think of me,

and it'll take you back to

every

single

one

of those ten years we spent together,

inseparable

and invincible.

Tell me—

after all this time,

how are you so

okay

without me?

And oh,

the words I would say

if I were just a little more

brave . . .

I'm the type of woman who brings

wildfires,

not peace.

But somewhere in those fires,

the right people

will find their peace.

And when it's finally our turn,
I'll walk up to you
and reintroduce myself,
"Nice to meet you,
I'm Forever."

—new beginnings

You caught me off guard
when you suddenly decided
to dance away with my heart.

Take my hand,

we'll see together

where this adventure may lead.

—starting over

Make no mistake,

my love will haunt you—

exactly as I intended it to.

I'm a lot to handle,
and if I'm too much,
you're free to walk away
and find less.

But less
will always leave you
wanting more.

In the dead of night,

as you lie awake,

do you wander back to me?

Does your hand wander

to my face,

the way you held it as you kissed me?

Do your lips wander

back to my forehead?

Does your mind wander

to every what-if?

I wish there was some way

I could convey to you

just how

beautiful

you make this world.

How wonderful it would be

if this were to be

our very last

first kiss.

I will continue to write about you—

for who you are,

for who you've made me,

and,

hopefully,

for someday.

—estrangement

Time

can take you by the hand,

but grief—

grief

will grab you by the throat.

Morning comes quickly

when you're in love.

Time fails to fly

without you here;

instead

it stagnates,

festers,

idles.

—grief

I'll meet you

in the cracks of light

at the break of dawn—

where we can surround ourselves

with forgiveness

and face the new day

covered in so much love

the way we've always known.

I see you in every sunset—

they were always your favorite.

What sadness,

to find something so

painful

in something so

beautiful

—grief is an ugly thing

The day I stop missing you

is the day I forget

who I am.

How strange it is

to return to our city

yet not fall in love with you again.

The way the stars aligned

just ever so perfectly

to give us this chance—

I will thank them every night

by loving you

with all that I am.

What an incredible gift to be blessed with—

the ability to love another

based purely on their soul.

If I ever am to lose myself,

I pray it's in you.

One day,

I will learn how to say

goodbye

without also leaving a piece of myself behind.

It's the way you know
how to stop my heart entirely
with just the touch of your hand,

the way your eyes
locked on mine
take my breath away,

and the way your kiss
brings me back to life
every time.

Isn't it funny?
I never did find myself
writing about you.

Take my hand,

and together we'll see

where our

(beautiful)

future leads.

You are all of my
wildest dreams
come true.

When the sun sets on our very last day,
I'll tell our story to the stars
as I grasp your hand in mine,
ready for whatever lie ahead
because of your love.

Old wooden docks

were made

for our slow dancing feet

as those north-Wisconsin stars

illuminated your face

in their beautiful glow.

To love a poet

is to know that,

at any given time,

the woman you've given your heart to

has at least ten ways to describe

the way your black hair falls in your face

every morning.

To love a poet

is to put your heart

on her typewriter chopping block,

to risk her words

for a chance that she'll turn that heart

into something that pierces the soul

in just the right way—

that you feel all the things you forgot how to feel.

To love a poet

is the ultimate game

of risk versus reward

because you know too well

what her words can do.

I was made for you

and maybe,

in some other lifetime,

you were made for me.

—timing

You were temporarily my forever,
and I will hold onto you
until my end of days.

With you,

I fully intend

to stay.

My favorite thing

I've ever been

is yours.

Maybe it's the way
her long hair blows
in the autumn breeze,

or the way the sun
dances
on her tan skin,

or maybe it's the way
those brown eyes glisten
in the October sunset

that makes me fall
a little harder
every day.

It's the way the

f i r e

in her soul

could burn this whole world

to the ground.

Maybe what I'm trying to say
is that I wouldn't mind
falling a little more in love
with you.

Your forever came

just a little too late.

And I could say that

I can't wait to come home to you,

but the truth is,

you are home.

When the sun rises

on a new tomorrow,

I promise I'll still

be holding your hand.

I think I could spend forever
writing about the way
her black hair
falls down her back like an ocean.

Even more simply,
I think I could spend forever
writing about her.

When the end of this lifetime draws near

and just the two of us remain,

we'll look back on every moment together

every laugh,

every kiss,

every sunrise,

and sunset,

and as we press our foreheads together,

we'll beg the universe

for just one more chance

to do it all again.

—soulmates

About The Author

Nikki is a runner, dancer, teacher, model, and traumatic brain injury and domestic abuse survivor from the Chicagoland area. When she isn't writing, she enjoys painting, traveling, and spending time with her family and pets. More often than not, you can find her on the beach or near the water. There are few things she enjoys more than hearing from her readers; you can find her and more of her work on Instagram @nixwrites_.

CPSIA information can be obtained
at www.ICGtesting.com
Printed in the USA
BVHW040700180222
629427BV00010B/407